WD

ACHOUNA
Boy of the Arctic

STORY AND PHOTOGRAPHS
BY DOMINIQUE DARBOIS

F Follett Publishing Company
CHICAGO   NEW YORK

and Fernand Nathan   Paris

LIBRARY OF CONGRESS CATALOG CARD NUMBER: 62-10391

THIRD PRINTING

Greenland

Baffin Island

Davis Strait

Arctic Circle

Achouna's Home

Northwest

Territories

Foxe Basin

Hudson Strait

Hudson Bay

Manitoba

Newfoundland

ASIA

EUROPE

North Pole

Greenland

AFRICA

Pacific Ocean

Arctic Circle

Baffin Island

Canada

United States

Atlantic Ocean

SOUTH AMERICA

Quebec

UNITED STATES

Ontario

St. Lawrence River

NEW BRUNSWICK

U.S.

©FPC

Where Achouna Lives

Achouna, the little Eskimo, lives in the far north. The Eskimos are a hardy people who have adapted themselves to the Arctic's rugged surroundings. Although the Eskimos have been influenced by today's inventions and customs, Achouna's parents still depend mainly on animals and fish for their food and clothing.

Today Achouna and his father are getting ready to go seal hunting. Before they can start on the hunt, however, they must make sure they have enough supplies. The hunt could last for days since Achouna and his father must spend a great deal of time searching for the seals.

Achouna is young, but his parents expect him to do a man's work. His father has wrapped their supplies in caribou skins to protect them from the snow. Now he and Achouna tie the bundles on the sled.

The sled is made of wood. Wooden runners are attached to the platform by means of straps. Sometimes the Eskimos put water or mud on the runners. When the mud or water freezes, the sled glides more easily over the snow.

Since it is very cold in the Arctic, the Eskimos must wear warm clothing. Achouna and his father are wearing sealskin jackets, called parkas, which have hoods attached.

Achouna also helps his father with the task
of preparing the dog team. Before they can harness
the dogs, they must check the leashes for rips.
Each knot must be securely tied and yet be easily
undone in case of an emergency.

Achouna's father throws a leash out like a lasso. The position of each dog in the team is shown by where his leash lands. After all the leashes have been thrown on the ground, they form the outline of a fan. The leashes are then tied to the sled.

The lead dog is harnessed in the first and longest leash. Then all the other dogs in the team are harnessed behind him.

The nature of the Eskimo dog can be savage like a wolf, but Achouna's father knows how to make the dogs obey. To make the team go forward, he yells, "Mush!" He also can command the dogs to go to the left or right. However, Achouna's father gives his orders to the lead dog, for this is the dog who guides the team.

Achouna and his father are able to take long trips over the Arctic because of the dogs. When they are traveling, Achouna and his father sometimes trot next to the moving sled. If they are tired, they ride on the sled.

The boy and his father leave the rest of the family to hunt seals. Their trip is long. They must go to the coast where water appears between the blocks of ice. This is where they will find the seals.

When they reach their destination, the two Eskimos get off the sled and start walking toward the water. They are quite careful where they walk. Otherwise, they could fall in the water or be carried away on a floating block of ice.

Fortunately they know the dangers of the Arctic and do not get too far from the dog team. As Achouna and his father walk over the ice, Achouna's father tests its thickness with his harpoon.

11

Achouna sees a black spot in the distance. This black spot is a seal lying in the snow. The hunt is under way.

So as not to be seen by the seal, who might plunge back into the water, Achouna's father has stretched a piece of white cloth on two crossed sticks. The two Eskimos hide behind it because they want to look like the snow.

They sit in silence and wait for a few moments. Then slowly Achouna and his father advance toward the seal behind the white shield. They are careful to move quietly. They do not want to draw the attention of the seal, who is basking in the sun.

The silence is absolute, and nothing seems to move.

When they are close enough, Achouna's father aims his rifle and shoots the seal.

The seal is a valuable animal. Its skin is used either for making clothes or dog-sled harnesses. The seal also represents real wealth to Achouna's family, for a sealskin can be traded for such important supplies as tea, sugar, and salt.

Besides the food a seal provides, its tendons are made into thread. The blubber, or fat, of the seal furnishes Eskimos with oil for cooking and light.

Achouna ties a rope around the seal and drags it back to the sled. Achouna does not have a difficult time pulling the seal because the ground is icy and slippery.

15

Seals can live on both land and water. When on shore they like to sun themselves or sleep. They are able to move on land by wriggling their bodies and by flapping their front limbs, known as foreflippers.

Achouna and his father have caught two other seals and now decide to return to their family. On the way back they talk about the hunt, the number of seals they killed, and the dangers involved in catching them.

For Achouna and his family, every day is a struggle against the cold. They live for most of the year separated from other families. They know that they can count only on themselves when dangers arise.

When they reach their family, Achouna's father selects a place to build an igloo. To the Eskimos an igloo can be any type of dwelling, not only a home. The igloo will be made out of snow blocks. However, igloos also can be made from stones.

Achouna's father starts to cut the blocks of hard-packed snow out with a saw. These blocks look like large white bricks. They are about two or three feet long and a foot wide.

Achouna has two brothers and a sister. One brother, Netcheapik, is four years old. His name means the "Little Seal."

Netcheapik likes to imitate his father by trying to cut snow blocks out with a knife. However, the blocks he cuts are not nearly as big or as even as the ones his father has done.

When Achouna's father has cut out enough
blocks, he begins to build the igloo with the help
of Netcheapik. He places the blocks side by side
in a circle to form the base of the igloo. Then he
starts to stack the snow blocks up vertically to
make the walls.

The blocks are placed in a slightly inclined manner. In this way the blocks are held together by their own weight. However, Achouna's father also fills the cracks between the snow blocks with loose snow to further fasten them together.

22

Little by little the circle becomes smaller.
After each block is placed in position, Achouna's
father smooths its edge with a knife.

The igloo is an example of how to build a
dome-shaped house without a support underneath.

The snow blocks are themselves slightly curved. This causes them to tilt inward as Achouna's father puts them into place.

Sometimes a block of clear ice will be placed among the snow blocks to serve as a window.

Achouna's little sister, Noonah, also wants to help in building the igloo. Her name means the "Little Earth."

Since it takes only a few hours to build an igloo, an Eskimo can travel across the Arctic without worrying about where to stay.

The igloo is nearly finished. Only a few more blocks are needed at the top, and it will be ready for Achouna's family.

Making an igloo is not as easy as it looks. The blocks are heavy and must not be broken when put into position.

26

Achouna's father uses his knife to make an opening in the igloo. Once everyone is inside, a slab of ice is used as a door to close the opening. The igloo gives the Eskimos protection from the icy winds of a blizzard.

Achouna goes inside the igloo. He continues filling the cracks with loose snow. The soft light which filters through the snow makes the blocks look like large, irregular stones.

28

Achouna's mother must get on her knees to enter the igloo. She is carrying Achouna's younger brother on her back. She has wrapped him in furs for protection against the wind and the cold. Eskimo children often travel like this until they are three years old.

The entire family goes inside the igloo. Achouna's mother uses a small sharp scraper to take the oil out of a piece of seal fat. The oil drains into a bowl placed at one edge of the board. She uses the oil to heat and light the igloo and to cook.

30

She pours the oil into a shallow bowl. The bowl is made of stone and is used as a lamp. The wick for the lamp is made from moss which has been twisted together. Achouna's family uses this small oil lamp to heat and light the igloo.

While his mother fixes the lamp, Achouna goes outside with a metal pot. He selects a clean spot where no one has walked and fills the pot with snow. His mother will put the snow-filled pot over the fire. When the snow melts, the water can be used to boil the seal meat and to wash themselves. When they are thirsty, they just suck on snow.

Any extra meat is kept in the snow. After each hunt, the father digs a deep hole in the snow. He puts part of the seal meat into the hole. In this way the meat becomes frozen and can keep for several months. When hunting becomes difficult because of bad weather or lack of game, this frozen meat will feed Achouna's family. Fresh seal meat is preferred, but in their struggle against hunger, this extra supply could save the family from starvation.

The snow is useful in another way. When the igloo becomes dirty, the Eskimo removes the dirt and replaces the damaged parts with clean snow.

Noonah is six years old and already knows how to be of assistance to her mother. Noonah spends most of her time with her mother, who has taught her how to cook and sew. The two of them now wait for the snow to melt in order to cook some seal meat.

After the seal is cooked, Achouna's father hands out pieces of meat to the children. Although they are inside the igloo, they still wear their parkas. Another way they keep warm in the Arctic is by smearing their bodies with seal fat.

While the children eat and talk, their mother makes sealskin boots. The Eskimo name for these boots is mukluk.

Before she sews the skins together, she softens them with her teeth. This task requires a great deal of patience, for it is a very slow process.

The upper part of the boot is finished with a band of wool upon which she has embroidered brightly colored designs.

36

After eating, the children go outside. On a
sealskin they play a game. First they put carefully
chosen seal bones into a mitten. Then they try to
get them out by means of a strap with a noose at
the end.

Each bone has a meaning. One bone can mean a snow block. The other bones in the mitten represent a person, a seal, a dog, and so on. To win the game, a player must get the largest possible number of bones out on each turn. Then the player builds an igloo, a sled, a dog team, or whatever else he wants to make.

Netcheapik shakes the mitten to mix the bones up. Then he pulls the strap out. Nothing comes out, and he must wait for another turn to get any bones. Achouna, a more skilled player, pulls out a bundle of bones.

Achouna has succeeded in pulling out enough
bones to build an igloo. He builds the walls of
the igloo with fifteen bones. Inside the house the
two bones on the right represent a seat. The two
bones on the left stand for his two brothers.

40

He places three bones across one bone to show where his mother keeps the food. The bone next to the food shows where his sister, Noonah, sits. The last two bones inside the igloo represent his mother and father. Outside the igloo the eight bones show where their dogs stay.

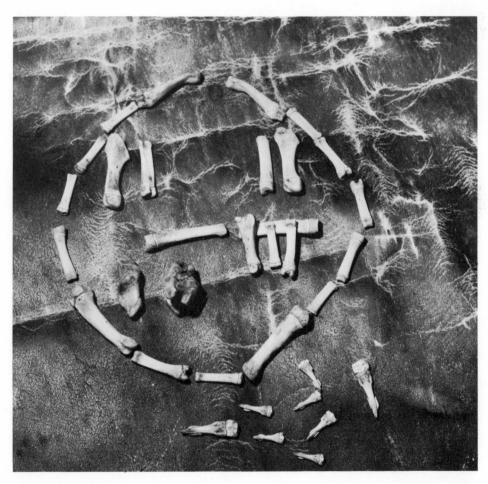

The wind blows very hard in the Arctic and carries surface snow with it. The dogs, who sleep outside, roll themselves up into balls to resist the wind. Little by little the snow-filled wind covers them up in a white blanket.

These dogs are of great value to the Eskimos. They are used to pull sleds, carry packs on their backs, and hunt seals and bears.

Eskimo dogs are known for their great endurance and courage. They can travel from fifteen to around forty miles a day, and a team can pull over two hundred pounds.

42

The children cannot sit still too long because it is cold. Noonah asks Achouna to take her sledding. Since she could not play the bone game, Achouna decides he will take the time to play with her. He gets the sled and pulls Noonah to the top of the hill.

When they reach the top, Achouna gets on the sled and wraps his arms around his sister. The two children start down the hill on the sled.

Noonah is afraid, but she is so proud to play
with her older brother that she says nothing. She
closes her eyes at times, but she knows that falling
in the snow will not hurt. For an hour Achouna
and Noonah go up and down the hill on the sled.

45

46

The children decide to go inside the igloo and go to sleep. They are tired after sledding for so long.

Their mother has placed a sealskin on the ground on which they can sleep. Two blocks of snow under the sealskin will serve as pillows. They also wear their parkas to bed. Achouna and Noonah fall asleep and dream of a country where they will find thousands of seals.

Other books in the series

HASSAN, Boy of the Desert

The fascinating story of a trip across the vast Sahara with a tribe of nomads

KAI MING, Boy of Hong Kong

An exciting description of life on a Chinese junk in the Hong Kong harbor

PARANA, Boy of the Amazon

The story of an Indian boy whose home is in one of the great forests of South America

RIKKA AND RINDJI, Children of Bali

The exotic story of children living on the island of Bali

TACHO, Boy of Mexico

The charming and colorful tale of a boy and his burro in a small Mexican village

TEIVA, Boy of Tahiti

A beautiful story of a Polynesian boy on the island of Tahiti

AGOSSOU, Boy of Africa

The delightful story of a boy who lives in a small village in Africa

NORIKO, Girl of Japan

The story of a typical day in the life of a young Japanese schoolgirl

LAKHMI, Girl of India

The work and play of Lakhmi and her brother in a holy city of India

WD